HELP

for the

VICTIM ENTITLEMENT EPIDEMIC

MARY NESTLE-HALLGREN

ISBN: 978-0-9655376-1-2

"What Would My Mom Do? (Drink Tab and Lock Us Outside)" Published on March 26, 2015 in Community Today, the author writes about the difference between parenting today and yesteryear. Parenting stress is higher and anxiety stems from "this notion that our kids' childhood must be Utterly Magical; a documented fairytale in which they reside as center of the universe, their success is manufactured (or guaranteed), and we over-attend to every detail of their lives until we send them off to college after writing their entrance essays"…in the old days, "They didn't worry endlessly, interfere constantly, safeguard needlessly, or overprotect religiously."

Contents

PREFACE

This book is intended for parents, therapists, and educators.

Through my practice in working with people's issues I encountered a very difficult set of people that I found extremely difficult to work with. These are people who insist on seeing themselves as victims in and of the world. This attitude is hard for people break in themselves as well as to change in others and almost impossible to work with. The person has to want help and if victims wanted help they wouldn't be victims anymore so they can't change. This victim perception seemed to begin in the generation at the beginning of prosperity. Everyone before that time, was a victim, but didn't see themselves that way. Things were so bad no one expected much and they appreciated what they did have.

I wondered why a person would seek therapy if they insist on holding this victim mindset. I finely decided it was because they wanted to be heard, or wanted validation and support for their victimhood, they need attention, or wanted sympathy.

Psychology may offer these rewards – Emotionology doesn't. Emotionology is about fixing emotions not just talking about them. I want the bottom line and get to the core of the issue. Emotionology is about fixing it by re-programming.

Victims really want help but want someone else to fix the situation for them while still not giving up their victimhood. That is impossible. They want you to change, they don't want to change. It is very important not to support this frame of reference.

I have accepted my learning journey with these people and hope my sharing it with you can save you some time and money.

INTRODUCTION

Victim thinking is blaming thinking and takes away the personal power of a person. A person needs empowerment, confidence that comes from faith and trust, and the determination to do whatever it takes to succeed. A victim won't look for this kind of empowerment. They will look to be supported outside themselves. They will look to be taken care of or have their feelings exonerated by someone else without changing them.

The new attitude society is now dealing with is a generation of entitlement thinkers that were told they were special, and that they deserve everything without doing anything on their part – the Millenniums. Although there are many children in this generation that are not like that, the victim attitude is so pervasive in our society that it has begun to generalize into all generations.

It seems the problem is a result of a combination of two things - our changing culture as we moved into a time of prosperity and the new parenting ideas. In the old days, no one told us how to raise kids. We learned through mistakes. We let them mostly raise themselves.

Millennium children were born in the late 80s. Not all of them take on the victim mindset but many feel entitled to have everything given to them. They were not taught to be productive nor responsible, making them not equipped for surviving today.

Many older people are having difficulty keeping up with technology as it changes so fast and they feel at a loss too. We are in the most difficult of times with several generations not equipped to cope.

I have a set of kids born in the 60s and another set born in the 80s. The changes that have happened through these few years are astronomical. Each has their own challenges, but, there is help out there. It takes a willingness to learn and change. It takes full personal responsibility.

People need skills to cope with problems like increased technology, more exposure online, increased cost of living, as well as loss of opportunity in the workplace. Many are disadvantaged. The previous generation that didn't know how to provide the structure nor had the ability to keep their word, adds to the problem with parenting.

Since our government is set up legally to support victims and society is exonerating that mindset right now, the victim attitude has become pervasive and I feel compelled to identify it, expose it, and write about it. I will also attempt to provide some ideas to help with this problem.

There is hope for people with a victim mindset but it takes some very specific understanding to work with these people if there is going to be any change at all. It is also very challenging for the individual to give this mindset up. I am hoping that sharing my experiences will inform you enough so you can protect yourself and not add to the issue. And, if you see yourself in this book, my hope is that you will see how counterproductive it is and commit to changing your thinking.

I have run into the victim mindset mostly since the 90s and I am here to share what I have learned. One of the most important things to know is that, victims make other people victims. Victims are dangerous to deal with. It is important to know how to handle situations with them.

When someone is playing the victim r not taking responsibility for their action, it needs to be confronted directly, and be sure they don't know anything about you that puts you at risk, as they will definitely use it.

Mindset

Victimhood is a mindset. If you perceive yourself as a victim, you are. No matter what happens to you, if you don't see yourself as a victim, you aren't.

Sometimes it is a game people play, and not a fun one to be on the other end, if you become a victim of a victim.

Taking the victim's negative blaming slant on life is a choice. Some people see themselves as victims, no matter how benign their life, and others, will never take that slant on life no matter how difficult.

Victim thinking is learned and supported or modeled from others. Some people get it by observing or modeling the behavior of someone else and identifying with them. Others, get rewarded one time and then commit to it. Maybe someone felt sorry for them and that attention cemented that idea within them. The reward might be attention, pity or money. It can be anything that feels good. Once rewarded, victim mentality really takes over.

I don't see it as an inborn trait, such as introvert vs. extrovert. It can begin at a very early age, sometimes because a child observes a parent with that frame of mind, and sees that behavior working for them. Most people develop the victim mindset later, looking back resenting what they were dealt in their life. Not everyone picks up this attitude.

MY EXPERIENCE

I once had a man who worked for me with no legs and he didn't have one ounce of victim thinking. He accepted his difficult journey and made the best of it. It almost seemed like he didn't believe he was disabled. He didn't see himself that way at all. He liked to bring me a cup of coffee and I was afraid he would trip and fall on the extension cords on the floor. But he had no perception of anything being a problem for him – and it wasn't. He believed he could do anything anyone else could. What you believe is true for you.

Then there is Katz. What I like about Katz is that no matter what, she doesn't play the victim. She is also willing to work on herself. Katz is immature, needs to set priorities, needs boundaries, doesn't know how to be subtle, doesn't respond to texts or calls unless she wants something, doesn't always listen or hear me, but when confronted, is willing to learn and comes from true generosity. She gets that life is a learning journey. It is a delight that she wants to make life better for herself by learning from her mistakes.

I could tell she wasn't a victim right off because she didn't complain – she just stated facts. She didn't feel sorry for herself. Yes, she lacked skills but was willing to learn. She also could say what had happened without drama and accepted responsibility for consequences, taking action right away to help herself.

We had a little altercation a while back that helped me know more about her. I lived with her for a short time. She came to Denver for a new job and didn't have all the upfront deposit but I liked her immediately and we worked out a payment schedule. She lost her job in 2 weeks but got a less paying one that same day with fewer hours. She is young and learning about life. At least she is trying. I wanted to support her zest for life.

I believe that people deserve a chance. The first thing I noticed was that she didn't have any boundaries as she let a bum into her space who wrote on my walls. We worked on her boundaries and being too trusting. She made other bad decisions. She had to take a bus back to Illinois to get her car as it broke down on the way back from a long trip. Kids are so adventuresome that they don't realize an old car might not make a long trip. She had to make a second trip to get it fixed and of course couldn't pay the rent. I didn't want to be in rescue mode but she was trying real hard to figure life out. Also, because she was open to developing her skills, I was willing to invest in her learning. She never complained. This is key. Complaining is a sure sign one sees themselves as a victim.

I did let her off the hook for some of the rent to move her out. I happened to have an office where she could hang out and sleep temporarily if she was subtle. Well, she wasn't subtle. Her stuff was everywhere. I had to get her out of there too. Her boyfriend was coming to Denver and looking for a job and they were going to rent from another person that I knew in a week. I let her move back into my place while out of town for a few days without realizing the boyfriend came with a dog. They didn't clean up after themselves and left stuff for me to move to their next place. She expected me to be upset so she didn't answer my call. I wrote her off for a while. Maturity requires learning many skills. It is important to know the difference between lack of skills and victim thinking. I put up with a lot with this person because immaturity is very different from victim thinking.

After I worked on my own issues dealing with her, I text her back that if she was willing to work on all the things that this situation brought up, I would meet with her when I had time. She could have taken the victim blame attitude and never talked to me again. She could have blamed me for all her problems. However, she worked on the issues and we remained friends.

Life is hard for some kids starting out these days and I understand that. The willingness to grow, to have a growth mindset, is what makes the difference between rescuing them and investing in them. There is a difference in facilitating someone growing up rather than rescuing them from themselves, with actions that cost you, with no return. Everyone makes mistakes when they are immature. There has to be some forgiveness and understanding.

I am sharing several of my experiences throughout this book.

Victims fool you

I am going to share a few experiences I have had with people that do see themselves as victims.

I had a rental situation that helped me learn more about victim thinking. I was sick and at the same time coming back from CA to move back into my own house. My renter was taking her good old time to move out because she had found out that I was sick and thought I wouldn't be there. It was after the first, although she had signed an agreement that she would be moved by the first, and she already had another place. There was no reason she left stuff behind.

She had pleaded with me to give her the deposit back so she could afford another place and although she owed back utilities, I gave it to her. Now I had no leverage. Technically I should subtract her utilities and have a month to return her deposit. I was doing her a favor. It was a little favor to me though too, as I really wanted my house back after 6 years away.

She had played the victim so many times before and it was so obvious that she created all her situations. I was just waiting for her to self-destruct – hoping she would move on quietly so I wouldn't have to evict her. She kept refusing to leave and begging to stay while pretending she really hadn't found another place. I eventually had to take all the legal actions necessary to completely remove her.

I see now how she played on our relationship because I had come to know her over the past 2 years of renting from me. At first I sympathized with her situation. I liked her and she was really good at building relationships. She was very good at pretending and treating you like a best friend.

Some people are very good at acting light and happy. They can appear very positive and really hide their negative victim side.

In our victim society right now it is really necessary to be wary and keep good boundaries with people. I had lost some boundaries with this person over the two years. She had a domestic violence situation with her boyfriend where she seemed to be the victim. So I took her side. Anytime you have to take sides you are entering into a dysfunctional relationship. Later she would say, "I have no friends, I am never safe" but, she put herself in those situations. My compassion had slipped over to sympathy and she was able to use me. In the future I repeated this lesson with several people before I learned.

Although I tried not to be the rescuer, there were situations that seemed appropriate to help her at the time. Looking back I see that I should have held a deaf ear to everything she said. I should have replied, "You choose him, it is up to you to find out what you are supposed to learn." Later someone told me that she was stalking the very guy that had broke her arm and

I am not sure if it wasn't her that was really the abuser. She was such a smooth talker. She could be so nice and sweet at times and I fell for it.

This was just part of my learning about victim mentality. Some people really know how to work your kind generous side. It is important to remember that every decision that a person has made in their life has put them where they are right now, and they have consequences to learn from, so don't offer solutions – allow them to come up with their own solutions. If you offer a solution they can blame you later if they have that victim mentality.

The victim thinking is so insidious that it is very hard to get rid of and often hard to spot. Our society supports this pervasive victim and entitlement thinking in so many ways. All victims think they are owed somehow. You aren't.

No you are not entitled. Life is always been hard for everyone in some way. Like it or not your life is the result of your choices. Your choices reflect the ideas (beliefs) you live by. If you can't make money at your job, you picked that job, and you picked that field. Try something else.

If you can't get a job because of your education, the only positive thing to do is to recognize that you picked the wrong education and work towards a new future with new learning and idea. Yes you picked it. Sure there should have been someone to guide you but there usually isn't. Pull yourself up by your bootstraps and move forward - that is the only way to grow.

I had another situation that had to do with victim and entitlement thinking. I had sent my friend Jenny to my favorite dentist because it seemed she was becoming a victim of another dentist. I really got suckered into this one.

My dentist is really a great guy and of course he is in business to make money. Somehow, she doesn't get that.

Initially she was negotiating for a discount and later found reasons to be unhappy; giving me a list of everything she had paid him, seeing if I would help her get a refund. This is victim manipulation. She had the idea that since I had referred her and I was her friend, that I should offer to help her get what she wanted. She expected me to take her side. She was trying to manipulate me to use my influence with my friend.

This is a side note of some dental info since my other life was in the dental field. When the gum around the tooth swells after a root canal, oftentimes the tooth will erupt a little, and then it hits too hard and may need adjusting. If you can't tell that yourself and don't speak up, the dentist won't know. It is up to you to be responsible for your own body. Pay attention. Dentists have lots of people they see and can't always keep up with what is going on with you individually.

Dentistry is not an exact science. Can you imagine trying to work in someone's mouth? In dental offices, the front office often doesn't know what is going on in the back office, there is lots of overhead, and they have to keep the patients moving to make a living. Insurance drives this industry now just like it has taken over the medical industry. Whether it is medical or dental, it is up to you to ask questions, pay attention to your own body, and follow your own intuition of what is right for you.

The bottom line is that she wanted something back for her pain and suffering. But mostly what she did was complain, expecting someone to offer a better discount.

No one can read your mind. If you want something you have to ask. Instead, she called up and talked to the office girl – they gave her a discount but not as much as she would have liked. She was still mad. She was still playing the victim.

Victims are always looking for compensation for their being inconvenienced in some way. They are looking to shift responsibility. Life has many inconveniences – it doesn't mean you are owed.

Fear of confrontation can make you a victim too. She didn't want to speak her mind, she expected him to read her mind. I intervened and let him know what was going on just because I knew both of them. He wanted her to be happy. It wasn't all about the money for him so he gave her more credit back and then she was happy and grateful. But, complaining and playing the victim paid off.

How does that really benefit anyone in the long run? We all like a good deal but there is a fine line between what is fair. Also, someone is in business to make money – not to give their time and effort away.

When I met with her, I asked what it would have taken to ask directly for a better discount and why she deserved it. Her response was that she had talked to two desk people and they knew she was unhappy, but didn't take any action for her. The issue is really about being completely upfront. Just because you complain doesn't make it clear that you want something nor is it a guarantee that you will get something. It just makes you look bad.

Many people get their way by complaining. Complaining is a symptom of victim thinking and part of the co-dependent model. It doesn't make anyone like you and if you do that with another victim you might get a shot in the head. A person with better skills could have said up front what they would have liked to have paid, and let the dentist think about it. If they both want fairness, it works out for all concerned. He had already told her that he would do the crown for whatever she expected but she wasn't up front enough to disclose what she wanted. It was her inability to speak her own truth that created a difficult situation. She almost destroyed my relationship with my dentist friend and I ended up feeling sorry that I had referred her.

There is a fine line between complaining and standing up for yourself. Know the difference.

RESCUING

Rescuing is how we enable victims and perpetuate dysfunctional situations. It is a way to support lack of personal responsibility and dependency. Every time a person is rescued from their own mistake, they don't learn from that mistake. They learn they are not responsible for the outcome of their decisions. Children need to experience consequences so they learn not to do the same things again.

It is very much like raising a two year old that you give in to all the time so that he/she never has to deal with his/ her own emotions, never has to suppress his/ her wants, will never believe you when you say "no", never has to grow up and take care of themselves, will never develop the skills they need to handle their own life, will never believe there are real consequences to their actions, and will always manipulate you to get their needs met.

All victims are looking to be rescued, compensated, and rewarded in some way. All victims are looking to shift blame. Victim and entitlement mentality are the worst problems in today's society along with co- dependence which almost everyone has.

I have personally recently learned a lot about these issues from my own personal experience. Perhaps I continued to bring this to myself because I was writing this book and I needed to understand all sides of the victim and entitlement issues. What you focus on expands.

Rescuing is a black hole. I have many friends that didn't plan well for retirement and because I am a generous person I wish I could help them. Seeing them as "in need of help" and feeling a strong emotion about it means that I still have something to learn about rescuing or giving too much. Anytime you rescue, you are at risk of putting yourself in a position of needing to be rescued. So, beware. Giving is different than rescuing. Be sure that if you are giving a handout or hand up that you are not hurting yourself as well as actually hurting them because they need the lesson.

Not everyone that asks for help is asking to be rescued. One of my closest friends offered to help with this book and offered more help than she later realized she wanted to do. I assumed that she did it because she wanted to. I didn't realize that she thought she needed to rescue me as she saw me struggling with creating the cover. Luckily we were able to talk about it and work that out. Givers are people that often over-extend themselves. I have done that. I have been a rescuer as well as an enabler in the past and had to fix that in me to.

Co-dependence

People can be co-dependent without having victim thinking. Co-dependent people have boundary issues, are either too dependent or too independent and the issue revolves around caretaking or wanting to be taken care of or enabled. Many of these people end up feeling like victims but it is a very large issue in our society and takes many forms. It doesn't have to include the victim or entitlement thinking and is not the main focus of this book but I will touch on it.

There are self-less people and selfish people in the co- dependent model. The self-less people are accustomed to giving and taking care of others while forgetting about themselves. The lesson is to learn to also take care of you first and let others have their own learning from their own decisions and consequences.

The lesson is to value your own journey and to value yourself. You are valuable just learning from your experience. You have value just being here having a journey. You don't have to do anything for others to have value. There is value in just being here.

The selfish people really know how to take care of themselves but do it in a way of being a "taker" or playing on other people's feelings to get their needs met, and will often present themselves as desperate to be helped or a victim of sorts, so others with a kind heart will come to their rescue. Some of them also are in their situation because they rescued others instead of taking care of self and are now in need. Some people play both sides of the coin.

While I was writing this book, I was looking for people to rent out some property. It is interesting to see how the Universe sent me people that represented what I was writing about. Malinda was so open and willing to tell her story. She and her husband were trying to make a new start. She had lost her baby to social services because of the domestic violence and a meth problem but she had been clean for quite some time and now had a good job. She was willing to work on her issues and demonstrated that. She was very good at making me want to help her. She was so earnest and positive. How could helping her not be the right thing?

I did give her room and she did some work on some of her issues. She knew that working on her herself was one of my requirements for helping her. Within a very short time the drama started. She wasn't upfront about her husband selling drugs and being involved with making counterfeiting money. They both had records. Can it get any worse than this? She was very good at lying to your face and playing this very nice good little girl. I should have done a background check. I paid for this mistake.

Of course, when I asked her to pick up her stuff the threats began. She was going to give me trouble. She had "rights". Where were my rights? Why is it that all desperate people are only seeing their "rights" and not the rights of property owners or people that try to help them?

Isn't this similar to those political people demonstrations where people break the windows of store owners and damage property, just to make a statement.

How is it not wrong for them to do all that to other innocent people? How do we let this happen in our society?

I can understand the aggressiveness that some victims feel. I needed a temporary membership with 24hr fitness as I was a few months between health insurance companies that usually include this. The sales person was very careful to state that I needed to cancel my membership by a certain date to be sure I wouldn't be charged beyond that time.

I took a special trip and went into the place with my daughter and cancelled a few days before the deadline. Then I went traveling. However, they charged me again as usual the $49.99. So I called them, told them when I had cancelled, and disputed the charge. They agreed that I had a cancelled membership, said they would refund and they did. However, two days later they charged me $39.99. I called again, this time they said my membership had not been cancelled and they would not refund the new amount. They offered to refund part after some discussion but I refused. I found myself determined to set this right.

Evidently because I had been with them through several changes they had multiple memberships from me that had been previously cancelled and so the person probably made a mistake and looked at an old one, so didn't cancel my membership when they said they did. Now it was my word against theirs.

Anyway, it took several people and calling corporate before they finally canceled my membership and refunded the money. It wasn't much money but I experienced the feeling that victims probably feel in that "I am right and you are wrong!" I had quite a bit invested as I had gone to great lengths to be sure that they got my cancelation on time and had also made two extra phone calls to check on this. "This was not going to happen!" I wasn't feeling victim but I was extremely determined in getting what I thought was right in this case. There was NO WAY I was going to let them get away with this. Because of my experience, I understand the determination that some victims feel to get what they want and what they feel is right.

Being "right" about something is a belief and when we buy into a belief we fight for it. Beliefs are hard to change because we are locked into an idea and have already made a decision. See "Emotionology's Ideas and Concepts" book about beliefs.

There is a powerful feeling that comes with being right along with the unwillingness to let go. Fighting mode is powerful. Sometimes principle seems more important than anything. Sometimes the determination comes from the investment already made. Often times, it is better to let go and not fight. But, there is a difference between standing up for you and playing the victim.

In my case, I was calling them on their mistake, taking action by asking for a supervisor that could make a decision, being clear about what I wanted, having evidence for my position, and not backing down. If I had the victim mentality, I might have retaliated just to get even because they were wrong in my eyes. In either case, getting what the person wants usually ends the problem. However, victims often are devious and carry the situation further even when they get what they want as they want to do damage to others. The problem is more global with victim thinking because they often see themselves as society's victim.

It is important to pick your fights. When we feel "right" it is very hard to let go. It is very hard to back down. It is very hard to accept what doesn't seem right. I didn't have much to lose with 24 hr fitness but sometimes it is necessary to look from a larger picture. Sometimes it isn't worth the trouble, time or energy to fight and that puts you into the negative realm of life.

When my old friend Joe texted me today, he shared how he didn't know how long he could hang on. He wasn't getting enough work to support himself. He didn't make much money and has a very small social security. He is living in his office and that situation is tenuous. He was tugging at the part of me that is helpful and generous. He is an old friend that I love. I found myself in anguish feeling for him and I wanted to find a solution for him or make an offer to help him. I am a person that always sees the possibilities and loves to partner and share a journey of possibility with people I like. Sharing a journey makes life so much more fun than doing it by one's self.

Several other friends the same day were sharing the difficulties they were having. I was feeling overwhelmed by the weight of all their needs. This time I worked on each situation for my own thinking and learning before taking any action. I could see that Joe needed to want more for himself and to want to provide a better life style for himself. He had made many decisions that gave away too much to his kids taking care of them, well beyond the age they needed him while not taking care of himself. He would over-give to people he loved. He didn't provide for himself.

After working on my own feelings around this, I asked him his options again. Could he live with his son? Earlier he said he really didn't have any options. This time he said, "I guess I could sell that piece of land I inherited and help my son buy some property upstate where they could have a shed for their old man in the back." All of a sudden he could see some possibility. Had I jumped to inviting myself into the equation of solutions, he wouldn't have come up with his own possibility. It is best not to right away offer a solution to someone that is in need so they have a chance to find their own solutions.

Finding your own solutions to your own problems is so much more empowering than leaning on someone or waiting for them to help you. Waiting for someone to help you brings out dependency and low self-worth. If I put myself in that situation it makes me want to cry. It feels disempowering. It takes away prosperity or abundant thinking. So if you offer to help too quickly, you actually trigger a person's dependent side, limitations, and scarcity. This is important to understand since you can be supporting dependency by being too helpful.

ANGER

Victims are usually angry. Anger is a secondary emotion after a judgment has been made. What I mean by that, is that, the person is holding some other feeling or idea and anger is the result. This initial feeling might be hurt or jealousy and then moves to anger. Anger usually comes after a person feels some feeling of unfairness.

Most negative feelings make you feel stuck. Anger is the only negative emotion that has movement and is more dangerous to others than yourself. Since anger moves one to action and if that action is against someone else, it can have repercussions.

Although anger is negative, in most situations it feels positive and motivational. For functional people it is often more useful than other emotions because it spurs one into action. Feeling anger feels better than feeling hurt as it is more self-empowering. Usually we feel anger because we have let some situation continue too long. You didn't speak up soon enough.

If you feel hurt, let yourself get angry for a short time. If you are functional, then decide what you have to do to fix the situation so you can learn from it to move on. However, anger spurs victims into action that is dysfunctional and hurtful to others. It is a driving force because it feels powerful and often pairs with vindictiveness. Anger often leads to retaliation.

For most people with a growth mindset, anger spurs them to positive actions that gets them out of some situation but if someone has a lot of self-pity, resentment, or victim thinking, they will complain, blame, and retaliate making victims of other people.

If you are an independent action oriented responsible person that takes care of yourself, don't expect everyone else to think like you. You have to observe people to learn how they think and act. Victims don't take responsibility for their lives and blame everyone else for where they are in life, so you might get trapped helping them because you made an assumption that they should be like you. This was my important lesson - I never ever felt like a victim so couldn't understand someone thinking that way.

The victim thinking can be very subtle and manipulative so one has to be very careful especially if you are a helpful person. Victims are takers and you might be being overly generous to the default. The pot fits the lid in that takers pair with givers and helpers attract takers.

Victims also may have just been a victim to someone else and then take it out on the next person they run into. Victims can also be givers and give away too much making themselves victims of themselves or give too much and then resent it later.

Most victims are coming from fear but they use fear and threats against others to get their way and get on top of the next situation. A victim might be feeling fearful but if they can switch places and make you afraid they will feel empowered. They often threaten others or act threatening because that works for them. Being a victim becomes a habit.

Sometimes victims don't have the verbal and communication skills to negotiate or speak up for them so that alone; can make them feel like a victim due to their lack of skills. They expect others to mind read for their welfare and then feel resentful because they don't get what they want.

Let me contrast two people named Judy and Nancy and explore their different thinking. Both women wanted the divorce. Nothing really bad happened like domestic violence or serious difficulties to either one.

The marriages of both just didn't work long term. Both got married very young and neither had the skills necessary to make a relationship work. Nancy can say, I ended up with 2 great kids. I learned a lot and if I had to do it over with, I would have left sooner. The other one has a completely different reaction.

Judy's x-husband tries to put a positive spin on it by saying; at least we ended up with 3 great kids. Hearing this from him makes her feel hurt and angry because, when it comes from him, she sees it as him justifying his behavior which is the reason she divorced him in the first place. She reflects on all the pain and energy she invested in that marriage for 30 some years. She reflects on what she put up with, all the meals she cooked, all the times he didn't remember her birthday and how he wouldn't grow up, making her have to grow up. She resents that she had to be the responsible one and be the one to discipline, make all the decisions, and doesn't get any credit for all the things she did. Do you see how she can only see from a very limited negative point of view which keeps her from moving on to the positive?

She is forgetting that she decided to marry the person for her own reasons. She stayed with him for her own reasons and lack of skills. It is a positive to have learned from that journey. It is a positive to finally get free of that situation. She could have made new choices earlier. She could celebrate her ability to be that responsible. She needs to see for herself that she did a good job and give herself credit rather than seeking for that outside her. Thankfully this person did learn to hold a different perspective. I congratulate her for changing the most difficult problem anyone can have. She had to WANT to do it – and she did.

Most of us stay in relationships that are not working way too long but however it worked is the way it was supposed to be. Once it is over, learn from it and be thankful for the learning experience and move on.

Relationships can be looked at like jobs, the first one you are the most inexperienced and have a lot of learning before you can apply for a new more rewarding job. If you take responsibility for your original choices, it is easier to realize that you can make a new choice and change the circumstances.

If a person has a few skills it is easier to move on. Sometimes co-dependence, not feeling independent, not seeing the big picture, not knowing one will be safe, not having faith and trust, is what keeps a person in a bad situation. I understand that it takes personal work to develop these skills. Sometimes the situation has to get bad enough to take that leap of faith. One has to still accept that it was their journey to experience, learn from, to move forward.

Anybody that isn't going to allow themselves to be a victim will make that choice to leave a bad situation because it doesn't do children any good for people to stay in an unhappy relationship. It isn't good for kids to see abuse. Viewing abuse, they grow up and become abusers themselves. It isn't a good life example to stay unhappy. So if that woman had enough knowledge, had enough independence, could see the bigger picture, knew she could be ok, had the skills to take action…I am not saying she did have those skills…she didn't have those things or she would have made a different choice earlier. But, see how our lack of skills can make us victims which is often behind the decisions made.

We are only victims of our own minds. So whether we have the skills or not we have to take responsibility for the decisions we have made and not blame others for our lack of skills and let go of the perception of being a victim in order to change. Victim is a perception – choose NOT to see yourself as a victim… say, "I can learn the skills it would have taken for me to move on sooner."

Most victim thinkers don't want to face reality. If they faced reality they would have to take responsibility, and then they would lose their victim status, which, they perceive as giving them power. They would have to take some action or do some work. If they don't take responsibility for their own feelings they can't change. If they did take responsibility for their own feelings they wouldn't be into blame. If they took responsibility and had the willingness to learn they wouldn't be living in resentment of the past.

You can only change you – not others. You can't force others to change. So, if you continue feeling bad, somehow in you, its ok, to have those negative feelings. Do you want to feel bad? Does it feel good to feel bad? What is the reward you get when you complain to other people? What is the reward you want when you tell others how hard it was for you and how bad you feel? Is it pity you want? If so, that is not love that you will get. Pity is pity, and love is not pity. Pity is degrading. Someone is looking down on you if they feel pity for you.

Maybe your parents had a wonderful marriage and your father appreciated your mother and then you married a man that didn't show this same appreciation. So you would grow up kind of expecting that every man would be like your father... and it's logical to think that someone should be appreciative. We always think everybody else is like us or like the parents we modeled. If you are an appreciative type person, you would expect that he would be appreciative. You would expect that he would want to do things around the house. You would naturally expect that he would want to take more action with the kids. And so when you expect that, you keep being angry because it's not there. Is that useful?

We all model our parent's traits. I modeled my mother's aggressiveness and her vagabond spirit as well as developing fear of her. Fire came out of her eyes when she was angry so I lived in fear. I had to work on fear as well as changing my aggressiveness to assertiveness so I could have loving relationships. I was programmed to passiveness because of her aggressiveness. So I had to learn to have a voice under some circumstances and fix my passiveness. I had to work on my vagabond spirit so I could settle down and live in one place long enough to hold on to success.

Life is a constant learning journey to overcome limitations. My challenge to you is to face your limitations and call for a session so you can overcome. Most Emotionology coaches will give an introductory session free so you can understand how the techniques work.

Emotionology is set up to make you independent as soon as possible. The model is to make you independent and free rather than keep you as a long-term client. You learn the skills to help yourself. We all need someone there to guide us in the beginning but shortly you can move free with new thinking and help yourself with the techniques you learn.

It is important to live and let live. Sometimes the part of your mind that is caught in needing others to be a certain way, will hold yourself a victim to them, not being that way you expect. You might need to get fed up enough until you are ready to let it go. So how long is it that you are going to take to be fed up before you can choose to move beyond it...before you will do the work to relieve your mind of that expectation? How long do you need to suffer before you will get out of that victim mode? How long will it take you to be realistic? We can't live with potential. We can only live with reality. It takes acceptance.

To a client who is working on appreciation and seeing herself as a victim: "OK so we can try a couple different things to get out of the victim mode. You seem to vacillate between two different ways of seeing yourself as a victim. On one hand you have..."He doesn't appreciate anything and that makes you mad" (he should have skills he doesn't have)...On the other hand you are feeling sad he is not there for you in the old family way (I should have had what other people have...life should be different). Both are victim perceptions. So that same part is vacillating between these two ways of looking at him.

So let's start with this...and a little bit of it is hard because only in your own mind, can you see what you really need to do. I can direct you, but it is your mind...I can't get in there and change anything for you...only you can change this.

Whenever we are disappointed it is because we had some expectation that wasn't realized. Some people when disappointed by their expectations, can really get angry. At this point there is an opportunity to either take the victim attitude or move into acceptance and carry on. It usually takes some mental work to move on.

If you are disappointed because you didn't get your needs filled, you are looking outside yourself to fill your needs, and that isn't healthy. Pat your own self on the back. Appreciate what you can do for yourself.

Needs are a bigger issue. "Needs" are like holes in a foundation. Needs that were not filled when you were a kid become like a faulty foundation that you build your life on expecting that hole to be filled later, somewhere outside you, because it should have been filled in the beginning.

We give children a pat on the back and say "good job" to make them feel good and motivate them. Maybe you didn't get that as a kid, so pat yourself on the back for making it through all those times by yourself. Do the inner child technique to fix this one.

Victim has a lot to do with being negative. Bill called me up today and was complaining about how one of his partners doesn't return calls and was going on and on about the situation. However, he has been complaining about this for months while taking no action. He could easily get out of that partnership – he has had opportunities but his own lack of action keeps him in the situation. Doesn't this make him a victim of himself? Why would anyone stay in a relationship if they have to complain about them all the time? There must be some reward. Some people just get off on people listening to them complain. What do you think is the reward here?

Meeting with Ellen alone we were to discover the game she plays with Josh and has played all her life.

Her mother played it and her grandmother played it. It is the manipulative game using anger, punishment and rejection to get people to come her way. It keeps people around her constantly off center because they don't know what to expect next. She is really sweet and nice when things are good, but if she can find something wrong, or Josh disappoints her in any way, she will criticize him to make him the bad guy, punish him for not being there for her, or not living up to her expectations, and reject him so he will feel bad and come to her.

Sometimes this is called BPD or borderline personality disorder because a person uses their anger to manipulate others in close relationships around them, to get their way. This game wouldn't work if the other person wasn't trying to keep peace. In this case Josh is dependent on Ellen being OK for his own happiness. If he was independent and fine with his journey, and knew he was really OK, he could let Ellen have her journey with her own emotions, and she couldn't play this game with him. He is just as responsible for keeping the game going as she is.

Ellen looks for things to be wrong so she can complain. She gets rewarded because he will try harder to make her happy. She would criticize him and since he wants to prove he is ok, he will try to please her. He is always walking on eggs, second guessing what she wants. When he doesn't perform to her satisfaction she will punish him.

Ellen can come up with almost any situation to see herself as a victim to get attention. One time they were trying to be friends so they were holding off sex so they could develop their friend part. They used to take showers together so she was in the shower by herself and started to get mad that he wasn't in there. So acting mad she went into her bedroom to mope and shut him out. He asked if she was OK and shutting the door on him was a way of rejecting him so he could feel bad and come her way – which he did. Playing this game is where one person uses rejection to make someone want the other person more. Have you ever been in a relationship where everything seems to be going fine and then the other person starts to back off so you move forward? This is the dance of negative relationships. Don't play it.

In life it is also about being right. Finding something wrong with another person so you can feel like you are right, is another angle of this game. Julie's mother finds something wrong with everyone else to put them down, so she can feel good about herself.

Our society is doing that right now against the police. If enough people can focus on what the police are doing wrong, that takes the focus off what looters and trouble makers are doing wrong. It doesn't matter how bad their behavior is, they can shift the attention onto any mistakes the police have made, to cover for what they are doing. The police should be held to a higher standard so this works really well. The game is to find the bigger offender and punish them. If society can punish the police for what they are doing, society gets away with what they are doing. If you can focus on someone else's wrong doing, you can take attention off you.

The key to recognizing this game is to notice people who criticize others, and who look for something to be wrong with others. They are usually negative to be around and blame others for what is wrong in their life. They often twist what you say to their own advantage. If you aren't afraid of their response they can't play the game. If you have anything invested in caring for their wellbeing, they can use it against you. If they have anything against you they will use it.

Then there are people who like to make trouble for other people. Parker gets a charge out of getting people in authority into trouble. He makes false claims against his parents, against the police to divert attention away from his illegal activities or anything else he might be doing that is illegal. He is a dangerous victim minded person.

Whiners and complainers are trying to get to you to make them happy. If you have anything invested in their happiness it works for them. They get what they want. Move away from these people and cultivate relationships with healthy minded people.

The thing is that you attract to yourself a journey to learn from, so... if you have these people in your life, it is necessary to work on the vision you hold of them in your mind, so you gain from that learning and attract different people.

My clients often find that they lose old friends because those friends don't want to change. But they find new healthy people as new friends that replace them.

Working with Shirley today we worked on her need to put other people down to feel good about herself. She remembered her childhood as everything being negative. She thought that everybody was better than her and that she was never good enough. She never got told she was good enough or did anything good enough. Her mother never told her she was OK and when she entered high school she felt everybody was better than her and that something was wrong with her. Even though she excelled in school and many activities and had friends, her confidence was temporary. If this is similar to your past, you can use the inner child technique to fix this. The feeling of not being good enough is a common problem to work on.

When a child grows up and no one tells them they are OK and everyone else to them looks ok, they often think there is something wrong with them. Later confidence that is built outside doesn't help the inside. It takes inner work to correct this. The opposite problem is giving children too much unsupported confidence. Telling them they are special and better than others can result in the entitlement attitude.

Today Judy had gone to dinner with a friend that told her she was a wimpy whining woman, is a waste of time, and thought she needed tough love. She feels bad because her friend doesn't try to understand and give her sympathy. I had to push Judy to work on this as she just wants to explain away the situation instead of fixing it. Turns out, it went back to her parents being too preoccupied, not realizing she needed their attention.

It was hard for her to change this. She still wanted to blame her parents for how she feels. Although it is true that her parents should have had more skills, they didn't. Every parent does the best they can with what they know at the time. Accepting this, helps one be open to change.

One man I worked with was working on how he felt about his divorce. He was trying to accept that marrying that person was just part of his learning journey. He came to a double bind. If it wasn't a mistake to marry her, than it was a mistake to divorce her. With the attitude that mistakes are just opportunities to learn and acceptance of one's journey he was able to corrects this.

These new constructive ideas need to be put back into old memories through one's imagination to make a correction in the body's mind to change the feeling. (See the Bio-Chemical Model for how this works).

Working with Katz is a very different story. We had that little situation a while back and she is willing to get the learning out of it. She realized that because she wasn't up front with me she felt like she lied. She had difficulty with confrontations with authority figures.

Her parents got upset one time because she didn't ask for time off from work early enough when they wanted to go on vacation. She was afraid to be up front for fear she would not get the answer she wanted so she just wouldn't talk. This has caused many problems for her in the past so she felt good clearing things up. This girl is like an uncut gem. Some of us are gems that were cut wrong – some just need refining, and some are really in the rough but all are gems.

Some people are very subtle victims…it is so hard to recognize it especially if one is looking for the good in people or assuming they are good. I had one person that tricked me for a long time because she would make her sob stories funny just so you would listen. Her reward was attention. But she never really wanted to change anything or work on anything. Her reward was attention.

Once again Ellen is feeling sad. She told me that when she told her story to someone and realized she wanted to hear back from them that they felt sorry for her. She wanted their sympathy. It sounds like an addiction.

People get addicted to getting attention, pity, sympathy, and many other negative emotions. This is because the victim is getting energy from others while they listen to the drama. Drama is the movement of limited energy. When someone is telling their story, limited energy is shifting between the person hearing the story and the person telling the story. Sometimes that is why a person has to top that story to get their energy back.

CONTROL

My son has been sick with strep a couple of times and we have a very strong connection and I love him very much. Because of this I was being over protective and constantly on him about how he was feeling and giving suggestions of what he might do to help himself get well. I was driving him crazy.

Sometimes when we love someone too much, we start controlling – at least that is how it comes off on the other side. It is actually a fear for what might happen to them that makes us do this. This over protective behavior is often what develops the polarity response in others.

Over protective behavior is very difficult for a mother-son relationship, when the son also loves his mother, and she is driving him crazy from too much input. It can become a love/hate relationship. It all comes down to responsibility. We have to trust that other people that we love can be responsible for themselves and that they know what is best for them. That allows us to let go as parents.

I was about to take a nap when I decided that my behavior with my son must stop. Of course, I would like my son to work on his side of it too, but that has to be his choice if he wants to learn from it. I lay there and thought about another person that I once cared a lot about but have completely let go of, how he ruins his health and how his health habits are so bad, and then I used a technique to put my son in the same place, as this person that I used to care so much about. There has to be a strong intention for this or you can't do it.

It is hard to realize that you can love someone so much that you start doing unloving controlling oppressive behaviors even though your intentions are good. Once I changed this, I felt real freedom but I had to change my behavior before he had the room to change his behavior.

I can realize now that he is free to get well. Without my changing my behavior it makes it hard for him to get well because he would be battling me all the time and have no room to think for himself or even know for himself what is good for him. Since changing this, I notice that my focus is more on me and my life. I can get back to living my own life instead of so much over-concern for him. After working on my situation I can recognize how I have several situations around me that are pointing to the same learning. I am human like everyone else and the learning journey never ends.

After working on this, I could see how I could still love him and let him have his journey. I could see how, I could now focus on my life. I could see how, he couldn't think around me. I could see how, I was imposing myself and my ideas on him. It had seemed like it was impossible not to care but now, I realized caring too much is not caring.

John is incapable of stopping himself from badgering his partner over his bad habits. He sees how his partner doesn't take care of his health and that it is breaking up their relationship. So he comments, makes suggestions, and can't leave him alone, which makes the other person do it even more. His partner has a polarity response so anything that is suggested, makes him respond in an opposite way. Over-care is caretaking and dysfunctional. We all need to learn to live and let live.

I had one client with a very strong polarity response to authority. If he told himself to go on a diet, he would do the opposite and eat like a pig. He would turn that polarity response on himself. A polarity response can be a big problem in the workplace. It prevents many from taking authority over their own life, because they are fighting authority outside themselves so much. People with this problem often can't take charge of their own behaviors. The polarity response is so strong it makes people do things they really don't want to do. It can be fixed though with the tools of Emotionology. I understand this as I had to fix that problem in myself.

I used to have a polarity response to anyone telling me what to do. That worked for me for a while, as it made freedom very important, and made me a good entrepreneur. However, it also made me have reactions that were not useful in my world, and I had to eventually work on this reaction so I wouldn't get myself in trouble.

Ed started a relationship with a woman that he is very much into sexually but she is negative and self-destructive. He wanted to prove to her that everyone was not out to get her. This is rescuing.

He didn't realize that he was replaying the relationship with his abusive victim oriented father who thought everyone was out to get him so he drew into his life a partner that represented his father's issue. We often bring to ourselves a situation that represents what we haven't learned from our parents.

Ten years later he now realizes this doesn't work, but seems unable to quit the caretaking and over-giving, which keeps this relationship in motion. He is a giver and she is a taker. Again this is, "The pot fits the lid." He rescued her, now...he needs to be rescued. His caretaker mentality keeps this in motion and caretaking is such a big issue that it takes quite a bit of work to get over.

When you rescue someone from themselves and continue the same caretaking and rescuing behavior that didn't work in the first place, you are feeding a black hole which is all consuming. The relationship will feed continually into itself and no one will recover.

In this case, she can't stop the taking behavior and he can't stop giving. After having a child, they are even more co-dependent on each other. When we don't fix something the problem will always get bigger. She doesn't want to work on herself because she would have to address her well paid victim status and give up being taken care of. She doesn't like her life, but doesn't know how to leave unless someone else comes along to rescue her and take care of her. She is very manipulative as all victims are. She knows how to get what she wants from others as all takers do.

These relationships are based on trades whether they realize it or not. All co-dependent relationships are trades. They all end, because, eventually one person gets tired of caretaking or the other person gets rescued by someone else. Some end, because, at least one person gets fed up or angry enough to leave or end the trade.

In this case, neither one likes themselves in this situation but they are helpless to stop it. She hates herself with the present person for having rescued her in the first place. She hates being dependent but sees no way to become independent. She doesn't want to work to take care of herself either nor does she want to fix herself either, as that would make it necessary for her to extend herself responsibly. Being dependent in the present situation is disempowering.

The sad thing is that a victim or an individual that sees themself as a victim, that is being rescued or taken care of, will retaliate if the rescuing stops.

EXPLORING PARENT CHILD CO-DEPENDENCE

There are differences between a co-dependent adult relationship and a parent/child co-dependent relationship but also similarities. The problem is that the parent who is doing the perceived giving and loving behavior is actually the perpetrator. The dysfunctional generosity, the over caring, the caretaking, the giving too much, the interference of taking personal responsibility by the other person, has to stop. The rescuing people from their feelings behavior needs to stop. Let them experience feelings. Giving in to tantrums has to stop. Giving in is not keeping your word needs to stop. Others have to learn how to deal with their own feelings preferably when they are young.

In the parent to child co-dependent relationship, the parent will never stop loving while making it so unbearable for the child that the child will end up sometime hating and will stay away from the parent. In romantic situations it just ends that they both hate each other and break up. All these relationships end disrespectfully.

The lessons are: You can't love someone more than they love themselves. You can't love someone into them loving themselves. Attitude is a choice. Emotional pain is optional. You shouldn't do more for someone more than they choose to do for themselves. Giving to a black hole doesn't make you a good person - it makes you the bad person. Giving too much takes the other person's journey away from them. It takes their freedom away from them. It makes them incapable of giving to themselves. It makes them incapable of helping themselves.

When a child has never moved out of the house or has moved back home and won't get a job or be responsible, it may be necessary to move them out to an inexpensive apartment and pay for 6 months upfront and leave it to them to sink or swim. Sometimes that is the only way or you will be paying for them forever. They will survive. They may need to go on government assistance as part of the learning journey. You may have to teach them about money first though before pushing them out of the nest.

Manipulation

Victims prefer to manipulate others to get their way rather than accept that they may have had anything to do with where they are. They don't easily want to learn from the journey. In the first place, in order to learn and see a different side, you must first accept some responsibility at being in a situation that has put you where you think you need to manipulate someone else.

The need to manipulate is trying to control others on your behalf because you refuse to accept what is and what you have done to contribute to the present. Manipulation is controlling and controlling others is not letting them have their own journey. Other people don't want to be controlled.

Remember, you chose to marry that woman that isn't what you want now. Your behaviors helped raise your kids. It was your decision to have kids. It is the sum total of all your decisions that put you where you are with your family.

Don't try to manipulate me to make your family behave in the way you want them to behave. That is not my role as a coach. My role as a coach is to help you see the mistakes of the past and learn from them. I can promise you that if you do that, everything will change. You can change the present relationship with your children and wife. You can change your way of being in the world so that you attract positive future relationships.

Mistakes are just part of the learning journey. Quit blaming others and manipulating others to get what you want. Blaming keeps you from growing. Manipulating others moves them away from you. You won't be happy. Find your way back to accepting the journey for what it is. Learn from mistakes and move on. Have faith, that if you change, others can change.

ENTITLEMENT

The entitlement I am discussing here is a mindset – not the government programs that give people a hand up so they can live or start over. Safety nets by the government are important to help people when needed.

Entitlement in this book is about a mindset that you are owed, without any doing for yourself, and where it is a misuse of entitlement programs or a form of mental illness that comes from enabling and dependency.

What parents need to realize is that it takes a burning desire to make it in this world. A burning desire must come from inside. You can't give it to someone - they have to give it to themselves. A burning desire is when you have a strong need that you intend to fill by yourself.

The things you have such as property, you have because you really wanted them. You probably wanted those things bad enough to get them at great effort. It took some action on your part. Or perhaps, you had no other choice. No choice creates a burning desire in some direction for most people.

If everything is given to kids and all their needs and wants are filled by you, why would they need to have any desire for anything that takes effort on their part? Why would they do anything for themselves if everything is done for them? When you give too much to kids it takes away the need for a burning desire.

Parents often don't realize the unintended consequences of loving and giving too much when it becomes caretaking. Part of loving is allowing kids to learn to think for themselves and be independent. Giving too much is not love. It's more likely to be a substitute for love.

Also, giving kids the idea that they can have anything they want, without any responsibility, and that they are special, and don't have to be responsible for their feelings, or actions, is detrimental to good mental health.

If everything is done for you without effort, how do you learn the joy of accomplishment? A burning desire and the need to accomplish is easiest learned at an early age. If a child is not allowed to think for themselves or do for themselves, and they are constantly being taken care of, to the point that they don't have to do for themselves or suffer any consequences of their actions, the feeling of entitlement sets in.

Look back at a 5 year old. Kids naturally want to be free and independent. What if this desire to be independent and free gets squashed? Would they expect you to be there for them and continue to do everything for them? When would it end? If nothing changes wouldn't they continue to expect that you will keep taking care of them? It is very hard to turn this around as they get older.

When you teach a person that they don't need to take care of themselves, how do you teach them that they do? They look at you and think "You are still capable of taking care of me, so what changed?" "I am still your kid even though I am an adult, why aren't you still here for me? "You brought me into this world, you are my parent, and you owe me."

The word "discipline "comes from the negative Authoritarian model or X Model. (See Emotionology's X Y System Model). Rules are made for kids. Discipline is necessary when a child is not obeying the rules. The purpose of discipline is to teach a child what is right and acceptable behavior in society and they experience consequences from any unacceptable behavior. Discipline is to teach structure. We want to teach them that there are consequences to their decisions.

In the old days we spanked small children. This worked only for very young children. Now days, other means are used. Now we need much better communication and structure to teach responsibility.

In the Y System "discipline" is replaced with guided learning and behavior change which includes a lot more compassionate communication. So the meaning of discipline has changed. A child at a very young age needs to learn what acceptable behavior is, and that you keep your word when you say "No". Your word is your integrity so if you don't keep your word the child grows up without integrity. You have to give a child structure so they learn to structure themselves.

A child needs to learn that tantrums, crying, and manipulative behaviors are not acceptable as a means to get their way. Giving in to these behaviors spoils the child in that they realize they don't have to change, since they can change you. A child needs to be taught respect and acceptable behaviors as well as consequences, through clear upfront communication at a very young age.

Does anyone change anything unless they need to? The first order of business is to let the kid know that your job changes as they grow up. Your job in the beginning is to carry them around until they can walk. Then you let them walk by themselves. You spoon feed them until they can feed themselves. You dress them until they can dress themselves. You cooked for them until they learn to cook for themselves. And, you financially take care of them until they are out of school and can get a job and pay for them. And the level of lifestyle follows the amount they get paid.

Missing any part of this growing up process sends a message that isn't congruent with a desirable mature result - that most healthy parents would want. It sends the message, "I don't want you to grow up and be responsible for yourself."

The next thing a kid needs to learn is the connection between doing and having. If they don't do anything, they won't have or own anything. A young person needs to see the steps it takes to get a life style they prefer.

Experience teaches best. Many things cannot be learned in theory; you must allow them to know the feeling by experiencing it. A child has to learn how money works as a medium of exchange. They need to change the medium of exchange they used to use, which might be, being a good kid, getting good grades, or looking beautiful, to get their way, into work action that creates money. This is a big shift and if a kid doesn't learn it they manipulate, steal, or become dependent longer than necessary. They need to learn what freedom is about....you are never free until you take care of yourself.

You are never free until you know how to be independent. You can't be abundance unless you are free. You want your child to be free, independent, and abundant. They will never be happy unless they are free.

How are you going to get this across to someone who is grown up already but never learned this? My youngest said to me once, "I don't want to grow up. It doesn't look like being an adult is much fun." He was about 12 at the time. Of course, I let him know that there is no other option.

Everyone grows up and you can make it a happy growing up or a difficult one, based on your choices. Most the time a child needs to leave the nest while they are still young enough to be adventurous.

If a person is already older and never had any responsibility or was never given the opportunity to grow up, it is like having a disability. You offered them a choice that even birds don't give their young.

If you had continued to carry the baby around past the time they wanted to try to walk, at what age would his/their legs quit being of use? If you wouldn't let them walk, the message is that they can't walk or shouldn't walk, on their own. In other words, take the easy way out and let me carry you. Then, how would you teach them otherwise when they are too big to carry?

If they had known only being carried and had accepted being carried around, they would be dependent on being carried. At the older age, their legs would be weak. They would need physical therapy. It would be a slow process. They learned from you they aren't capable of walking. And they wouldn't be. They would blame you for their disability. It might even be called child abuse. Did you need to carry them because that gave you value? "You did this to me and now I don't know anything else." How would you answer? "Why didn't you let me learn to walk?" "Why didn't you help me sooner?"

Now you have a situation that is abnormal. You have created an abnormal child's adult life. The little bird sat in the nest too long and you can't kick him out because you know he/she will fall. Birds know when to push their babies out of the nest. If they allowed them to freeload they wouldn't be able to raise the next set of babies. It is not natural to keep taking care of babies past the time they can care for themselves.

Change takes firmness and education. When you make someone dependent on you, you are just as responsible for the outcome as they are. Most often the parent needs a therapist, so they get the skills needed, to teach the child in a different way. They need the ability to let go. The parent needs to learn how to make a plan and keep their word.

The parent has become responsible for the child's behaviors and the situation as it is, so new skills are required to grow up the child at an adult age. The parent has been overly responsible for the young person too long, and the new learning that has to take place, is to teach that child self-responsibility and how to take responsibility for consequences.

It is part of survival in the world to learn all these steps. Everyone has to learn how to survive, and they don't learn it if they are never put in a situation where they have to survive.

A parent must show trust in their child's journey and give them the space to learn. This might include failing and they need to know that they will still be loved, even if they fail. Love doesn't come from being a success. Love should be unconditional. And love doesn't rescue.

Some children will not try because they are so afraid of failing in their parents eyes that they end up failing anyway. Fear of failure is a self-fulfilling prophesy that is driven in the sub- conscious. When a parent puts so much emphasis on success, that it feels conditional for their love, a child doesn't have the freedom to learn how to be independent. Change the idea of failure to mean only a learning experience. Support them in any difficult learning experience, but let them have every experience to learn from.

People fight change unless it is interpreted as something positive. From a customer, "Oh, you want to give me an even better price?" From an employee, "Oh, you are going to pay me even more for sitting on my ass? I am delighted." You are being so good to me. From the adult child, "Oh, you are going to pay my rent, give me a car, and buy my food. You are such a great parent." You might think the response would be, "Thanks, I love you." Instead entitlement thinking is more like, "You didn't get the kind of sauce I like. Why did you buy a Ford, I wanted a Jaguar."

Kids lie around and don't help out with the house because it's not their house - it's your house. If they felt invested in the family home by helping to take care of it, they will have a realistic vision of what it is like to own a home of their own. They need to see that a house is a responsibility – not just a place to hang out. They have to be taught to respect you and your space as they will want you to respect theirs. Respect is taught.

Most kids have to learn how to keep a job and manage their money. They need to know it isn't failure to have to start over or find a new job. They need to be OK to start at the bottom and work their way up. They have to learn to suck in their belt so they can afford themselves.

How can a child love and respect themselves if they accomplish nothing? How would they find their value if they don't do anything? If they don't respect themselves or their lifestyle they won't respect others. You have to respect yourself to respect others. If they don't like themselves, they won't be likeable or like others.

By the time children are 25, if they haven't learned to do for themselves, they are so behind other successful adults that they can't seem to catch up. They end up hating themselves. They will compare themselves to what others are doing at their age and feel inferior and feel like a failure.

The only thing they will know is that they are being taken care of and since they don't know anything else, they will fight to keep that going through manipulation and coercion. Be sure you can afford to pay for them the rest of their lives because when you die, they will have to fend for themselves.

Adult children living at home is a common problem in our society right now because of rampant co-dependence and treating children in an indulgent and over-protective way. There is a misinterpretation that filling needs and giving in to wants, equals love. But it's not - need is need and love is love.

A parent needs to love their child enough to let them do for themselves. You may need to love them enough to allow them the experience to live on the street so they want actually want to work.

There is an alternate side to the above situation though. If parents are rich and will always be able to afford to have someone never learning to be financially responsible for themselves, and the child is truly happy with that, perhaps it is OK. Perhaps that child's journey is to come into this world to experience a life of freedom from responsibilities. Who is to judge, if it is working for everyone and they are happy? We all choose a unique individual journey here and if what you choose is working for you, go for it.

Friends and lovers or partners can have a similar problem with dependency. You might be the one that is helpful and always taking care of others. You are teaching them that it is your job to take care of them. Do this too much and you take away their own desire to fill their own needs.

If you are always giving, they begin to expect you to continue being the way they experience you. When a person is on the receiving end of long term over giving, it not only is expected but becomes entitlement. You have treated them that way and they are entitled to keep having you treat them that way. They become a victim of your giving and become dependent on you. Some relationships become reciprocal - the more you do for them, the less they do for themselves.

If you are the person doing all the giving, you probably wouldn't let others give that much to you and so you don't understand when others do all the taking. You want to take care of yourself. You don't want to be taken care of. You have too much respect. You expect others to be like you. So it is hard to understand that someone would accept beyond what is healthy or mutual. It is hard to understand that someone would want to be dependent.

When you are in a situation where the giving has begun to be unhealthy and one sided or you can see that they are letting themselves be dependent, it can be very frustrating and hard turn around. Most of the time one has to get angry enough before putting a stop to it and cutting off the purse strings or rescuing that person. You have to be mad enough to totally let go of any of the consequences they created for themselves. If you work on this, you can make the transition easier.

We all can see the potential in others. However if they can't see their own potential or want to rise to that potential, there is no helping them. You can't live with potential. You have to live with reality.

Look at how this idea translates to society and the welfare system. We believe everyone deserves a home and food and they do but not without any action on their part. Government starts taking care of people. What would make anyone want to give that up? How do they if there is no bridge to independence?

There is a large group of people that are so defeated by the economy, their jobs, and how they can't make it in life, that they are miserable and have allowed themselves to be dependent on government handouts. They see themselves as victims and focus on the negative. Our government has created this outcome. Although giving is well intentioned, it has become dysfunctional.

There is no hope if you don't believe in yourself or believe in opportunity. However, there are always those who survive and thrive. There are always those who are optimistic and find a way to better their lives. Entitlement and victimhood is a mindset that is taught accepted or modeled. The ideas and lack of personal responsibility which has been learned has to change before change can happen.

Everyone does the best they can as parents. We were not taught how to parent. And, we can learn a new way to recover from situations.

What has contributed to so many adult children living at home? One is the opportunities are more difficult to navigate with our changing world. And, the larger society has changed parenting ideas that don't work for the highest good of everyone. Anyone can justify a negative attitude and the victim mentality because the world is hard. However, is that really useful? There have always been difficult circumstances in the world. There have always been hardships. Yet some people always make it.

No one is entitled to make it without helping themselves. And they need to learn how to help themselves through the right channels. Some learn to help themselves by taking from others. Usually this is because they don't see a better way. They might not know how to go about helping themselves or they are too addicted to the easy way out. At any rate, they have to WANT to help themselves. It takes an educational process to move people out of dependency and victim thinking.

You might resent that you don't have a better life, better pay, and better working conditions. It is up to you to create a better life for yourself. It might be you have to be entrepreneurial. You might need to develop some skills. It might be that you have to ask appropriately for what you need or want. You are entitled to go to a different company or be in charge of any changes you make in your life. You are entitled to make new decisions for your life.

People don't always get an entitlement attitude because they are spoiled. Sometimes they just pick it up from other kids or some negative experience that they generalize. No one comes into the world as a blank slate. There are personality beginnings with natural skills and lack of skills. Some babies come into the world with a negative slant as well as some who come into the world always seeing the positive or optimistic side despite their circumstances. There are other influences that are stronger than parents as children grow up. It is not about fault.

If you find yourself in any of the above situations, assess where you are and start taking steps to remedy the situation. Get advice from others. Ask yourself what you were trying to learn so you can learn that and move on.

Life can be hard for everyone and they need to realize that they are not the only one having difficulties. It is how one approaches those difficulties that create a different outcome for some. Buying into the victim thinking makes a person a victim. Entitlement thinking is victim thinking.

Give to others carefully and don't over give or over care. Sometimes the other person feels obligated or guilty if you give too much. A client that is also a friend came bearing gifts. Then she offered to pay an air fare for me with her miles. This person is very generous but I had to stop her. How could I feel good about charging her for my services if I accepted too much. It wasn't balanced. We had a talk about it and she understood.

Caretaking is doing more for someone than you should so that they don't have to be responsible for their own care. It is also giving too much of what you think they need, which might not be what they really want. What does it mean to someone else if you care take them too much? Doesn't it mean you think they are incapable?

When you care take others and give things they don't ask for and don't want, they have a hard time appreciating the gift, because you assumed. What is it that you want to experience in return? What is your motivation for caretaking someone else? What is your belief that keeps you doing this? What is the outcome you are trying to control?

If your kids didn't turn out like you expected, don't blame yourself for everything. Kids make choices too and it is their responsibility to how they live their life, so let go. As parents, we all want the best for our kids. It is a difficult thing to let go of their journey and let them make bad choices. It is so hard to watch. But, if you let them experience consequences early in life, they will do better later in life.

What I have learned from my clients and my own life, is that parents sometimes need to work on themselves so they can let go of responsibility of their child's journey. We love our kids so much. Once a child is old enough to start making decisions for them, they need to also be taking responsibility for all consequences of their choices good or bad. The parent needs to learn a bigger kind of love that might be interpreted as lack of love or tough love from their kid's perspective. If it goes on too long and the parent gets mad, the situation becomes authoritarian and threat based. It is best to get the inner strength to lovingly hold the line as one slowly lets go while they grow. Improve the quality and quantity of communication. Life takes explaining.

In Conclusion

One of the problems in our society is that there is no bridge to get people off programs and back independent. If a person on welfare makes any money, they might lose their benefits.

I was talking with a friend that has a daughter who is handicapped. If she makes $2, she only gets to keep one. When you receive social security, if you make money you might lose your social security. Do these programs encourage a person to be independent in society? Are they working?

I propose an educational program for emotional skills that has a firm structure to move them forward. Allow people to make some money without punishing them. Hire people to guide them onto an independent future with the help of developing their skills through Emotionology tools and techniques.

Without this bridge, society will have more and more people abusing the system because there is no other way for them to take care of themselves. What will that future look like? Let's create bridges to individual freedom, not just in government situations, but also in our personal lives. Everyone needs to live coming from a position of freedom and abundance.

I am done with the victim problem in my life as I finish this book, I have lost two of my best friends because they turned their victim thinking against me. It is amazing how subtle victimhood can be. But I have faith and trust in the part of them that is goodness, and if I hold this goodness in mind, over time, I know they will come around. Our relationship will never be the same unless they work on their stuff. In the meantime, I have learned so much in the process of working through all my feelings that I live in gratefulness and appreciation.

What I tell my clients that notice that they are losing friends, "It is because you have changed. The same people no longer fit. You will lose those who support your old limited self and old model of friendship. New friends will replace old ones in time." I have noticed this so many times with clients that I have faith in that for myself. I want growth minded friendships. I want people in my life who welcome change.

This is Farwell to victims…

THE OZ PRINCIPLE - THE DESTRUCTIVE FORCE OF VICTIMIZATION

By Roger Connors, Tom Smith, Craig R. Hickman Excerpted from March 2, 2010 from http://www.eno-talone.com/article/6584.html

Most people in organizations today, when confronted with poor performance or unsatisfactory results, immediately begin to formulate excuses, rationalizations, and arguments for why they should not be held accountable, or at least, not fully accountable for an organization's problems. Such cultures of failed accountability or victimization have weakened business character, stressing ease over difficulty, feeling good over being good, appearance over substance, saving face over solving problems, and illusion over reality. This trend toward victimization will only further weaken business character, deluding business leaders into providing quick fixes over long-term solutions, immediate gains over enduring progress, and process over results. If left uncorrected in an organization, victim attitudes can erode productivity, competitiveness, morale, and trust to the point that correction becomes so difficult and expensive that the organization can never fully heal itself or its people.

www.ingramcontent.com/pod-product-compliance
Lightning Source LLC
Chambersburg PA
CBHW071642050426
42443CB00026B/867